TRU

A

pι

ι

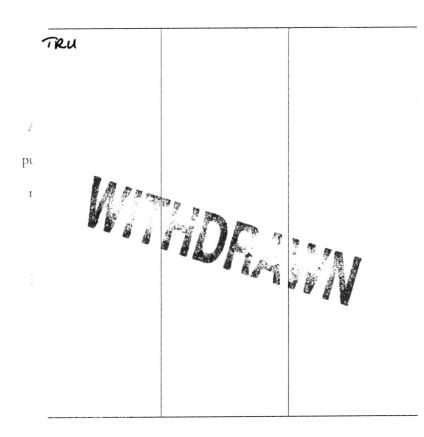

1

What is Post Traumatic Stress disorder (PTSD)?

As explained by Combat Stress: '*PTSD is a complex and debilitating condition that can affect every aspect of a person's life. It is a psychological response to the experience of an event (or events) of an intensely traumatic nature. These type of events often involve a risk to life – one's own or that of one's colleagues.*

It is a condition that can affect anyone, regardless of age, gender or culture. PTSD has been known to exist since ancient times, albeit under the guise of different names.

During the First World War it was referred to as "shell shock"; as "war neurosis" during WWII; and as "combat stress reaction" during the Vietnam War. In the 1980s the term Post Traumatic Stress Disorder (PTSD) was introduced – the term we still use today.

Although PTSD was first brought to public attention by War Veterans, it can result from any number of traumatic incidents. The common denominator is exposure to a threatening event that has provoked intense fear, horror or a sense of helplessness in the individual concerned.

The sort of traumatic events that might be experienced by members of the general public include physical assault, rape, accidents or witnessing the death or injury of others – as well as natural disasters, such as earthquakes, hurricanes, tsunamis and fires.

In the case of Serving personnel, traumatic events mostly relate to the direct experience of combat, to operating in a dangerous war-zone, or to taking part in difficult and distressing peace-keeping operations.'

Words of a Wolf

Poetry of a Veteran

Words and images by

Villayat SnowMoon Wolf Sunkmanitu

Foreword by Derek Thompson

Before asking the question,

ensure you have the courage to hear the answer.

SnowMoon Wolf

Foreword

The thing that stood out for me, from my very first meeting with Villayat, or 'Wolf', as he walked around the room in his baggy shorts, was an intensity that bordered on unsettling. It was as if he was struggling with some inner turmoil that he couldn't describe. What drew us together – then and now – was a desire for social justice. I didn't know at the time just how personal a mission it was for him or what lay at the heart of it. Post Traumatic Stress Disorder (PTSD) was just something I'd vaguely heard of and associated with the two world wars.

He can be a man of extremes – insightful and wise one day, brooding and defensive the next. What you see is what you get – there's not much filtering going on. I've seen him in good spirits when his laughter shakes the room. And I've seen him in difficult times, pacing up and down like a trapped animal, unable to express the pain and pressure that bursts through in aggression or confrontation or hopelessness. I've watched and felt inadequate – not knowing what to say or what to do. So I've learned to listen without judgement – as he's revisited old wounds or asked questions that neither of us could answer. In those times he's always anxious to understand why situations have recurred or unravelled, and even more anxious to avoid those same experiences in the future.

But, as Villayat has told me himself, knowledge will only get you so far – it doesn't change the instincts, moods and thought patterns that govern much of our behaviour. The kind of healing that reaches that deep takes time, space and professional care. It's something only the sufferer can instigate by daring to reach out and trust. This book is part of that process for him and I salute his courage.

In his writing you'll find a rawness and honesty that we're not used to in society, as well as some uncomfortable truths. Stick with it though because the reward is a deeper understanding of the lives of ex-servicemen and women – about what can happen when the parades are over and the uniform comes off but the damage is still there. It will give you an insight into their relationships and family dynamics too, and maybe why so many of them fall apart.

Villayat's quest for meaning, healing and peace of mind has led him to the traditions and practices of Native American culture. It may not be your path but you are welcomed here as an honoured guest, without judgement. I trust you'll treat my friend's invitation and his personal truth with the same open-mindedness and respect. And I hope you'll remember that – like so many other sufferers – PTSD continues to affect his life and his relationship with family and friends on a daily basis.

Derek Thompson 2010

Oh, Great Spirit – Lakota Prayer

'Oh, Great Spirit,
whose voice I hear in the winds
and whose breath gives life to all the world, hear me.
I am small and weak.
I need your strength and wisdom.

Let me walk in beauty and make my eyes
ever behold the red and purple sunset.
Make my hands respect the things you have made and my ears sharp to
hear your voice.

Make me wise so that I may understand
the things you have taught my people.
Let me learn the lessons you have hidden
in every leaf and rock.

I seek strength, not to be superior to my brother,
but to fight my greatest enemy – myself.

Make me always ready to come to you
with clean hands and straight eyes,
so when life fades, as the fading sunset,
my spirit will come to you without shame.'

Chief Yellow Lark, Lakota Tribe

Introduction

'Words of a Wolf' is a collection of poems that I have written as a form of therapeutic self-expression, to help myself cope with Post Traumatic Stress Disorder (PTSD), as well as the other everyday aspects of my life.

I served in Northern Ireland with the RAF Police from 1983 - 1985 and I'm still affected by the stresses and strains of my time at RAF Bishops Court. The condition wasn't diagnosed until 1995.

My poetry allows me to hang on to parts of my persona that might otherwise have been swallowed up by the PTSD, leaving me completely at the mercy of a debilitating condition, while the photography sets me free for a while.

The name SnowMoon Wolf was given to me by a teacher of the old ways from North America. I learnt how to cope with PTSD by using sacred herbs and ceremonies, guided by different teachers on my travels to some of the many tribal lands on the North American continent. I have been welcomed by Navajo, Hopi, Apache, Blackfoot, Comanche and Zuni people but the Lakota have a special place in my heart.

I was taught that the medicine I carry as a wolf is that of a pathfinder, protector and teacher. I have spent time with, and photographed, wolves in several countries. They've always filled me with a sense of wonder and peace. It was my passion for the wolf that kicked off my thirst for travel photography, which became my main coping mechanism for PTSD.

I dedicate this book not only to veterans but also their loved ones, who have the courage to stand by those afflicted by this condition, and have not given up on them.

I also dedicate this book to Joshua and Laila and to the other special people in my life that have sustained me with their friendship and love, to Derek for listening without judging … and to the beauty and medicine of the wolf.

I hope that you will enjoy the words and the images I have added from my photography career as well as the odd shot from the past - from those days in uniform that have been sat in albums, gathering dust over the decades. Most of these images can be found on my website: http://www.wolf-photography.com.

The label of PTSD scares some people and they don't know how to communicate with sufferers, which in turn leads to veterans being ostracised and not getting the care and support that they need and deserve. People are curious about our lives but don't always like the truth that our words and experiences reveal.

Villayat SnowMoon Wolf Sunkmanitu

For the one to come

I can't ride a horse,
But I'll be your warrior and slay your demons.
I'm not much of a gardener,
But I'll grow you a rose as best as I can.
I can't weave a blanket,
But the love I send you will keep the chill away.
I have my weaknesses,
But I'll take courage from your smile and overcome
them.
I have no use for wealth,
But I'll treasure your heart.

When I roam over the land of the wolf, I take you with me.
When I soar over the cliff and beyond the sea,
Your spirit is with me.
Every sunset I watch, I share with you,
Knowing that a sunrise of hope is only a few hours away,
I'll guard your sleep.

I have my darkness,
But I'll let you wash over it with your light.
I can't build a lodge,
But I'll protect you in my embrace.
I'm not a good painter,
But I'll let you add colour to my life.
Where there are no words,
I'll listen with my heart.

When I roam over the land of the wolf, I take you with me.
When I soar over the cliff and beyond the sea,
Your spirit is with me.
Every sunset I watch, I share with you,
Knowing that a sunrise of hope is only a few hours away,
I'll guard your sleep.

Set yourself free and teach me to fly with you,
Be who you want to be and show me the wonder of you.
Let your inner child free and teach me to play,
Come and dance on the wind with me and place your hand in
mine.

When I roam over the land of the wolf, I take you with me.
When I soar over the cliff and beyond the sea,
Your spirit is with me.
Every sunset I watch, I share with you,
Knowing that a sunrise of hope is only a few hours away,
I'll guard your sleep.

The sun sets and rises and you'll come when you can,
I'll wait until then.

Will You?

Every night before I sleep I think of you and send you
warmth,
Every morning that I wake, I wish to see your smile.
Every time I walk by the sea, I wish I was sharing the walk
with you,
Every night when alone by the fire, I wish I was sharing the
silence with you.
Every time I see something that makes me smile, I wish I was
sharing the smile with you,
Every time I laugh out loud, I wish you were there to laugh
with me.
Every time I long to feel a hug or a touch, I wish it was from
you.
Will you come into my waking life as well as my dreams?

In my son's eyes

I see joy and innocence,
An open spirit unhindered and unfettered by society.
No doors are closed to him that his smile can't open.
With his joy I close my childhood circle and celebrate his
freedom and growth,
And send a prayer to protect and guide him on his journey.

Gift of the Daughter

She's always been a ball of energy,
Bouncing at play from the very first efforts at movement.
Clear eyes showing a soul so pure, yet holding mischief in the
twinkle.
A heart caring and thoughtful, caring for me without totally
understanding,
Yet making all my cares fly at the flash of her smile, her kiss
or her touch.
Beneath it all lies great strength, created of love and
ancient wisdom.

You don't need a Facepack

Beauty is skin deep, yours goes beyond,
Lines are just markers that remind you of a number,
All the lines fade when people see you smile,
Because all they see is the radiance of that smile.
They see the soul behind it,
Connecting with your warmth and energy,
Knowing that in you they've found a gem.
So forget about the number and celebrate your wisdom
and the beauty that you radiate, and remember ...

You don't need a facepack .

Connected

I see light in the dark
I see a drink in the rain
I feel a caress in the wind

I feel warmth from the Sun
I see the tide of life in the Ocean
I see another year in the young buds

I feel awe when seeing the Moon
I feel the rhythm when I dance
I see life with my eyes

I feel the love of my cubs
I see the feather and the tree
I feel Connected

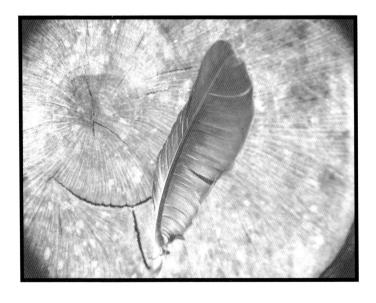

Choices

You're approaching a fork in the road,
Which way will you go?
Freedom or pain, sunshine or grey?
Pain is your partner but not by day,
As your smile hides the anguish reserved for your bed
But compared to living it's the easier choice.
Where will you go now ...

Sunshine or grey?

Province of Dreams

Memories of uniforms and rifles, bricks and bottles.
Mates suffering in silence, on the edge.
VCPs, patrols, stop and searches.
Invincibility of youth cloaking fears of death.
Staring in the darkness, waiting for the round,
While your oppo freezes and goes to the ground.
Memories of racism going unchallenged,
Until your mates spoke up.
Memories of piss-ups and the darkest of humour,
Dealing with the fear as if it's a tumour,
Leaving you cold, functioning like a machine,
Until you wake up with a silent scream.

Tears fall on your pillow.

Memories of the time when your two years were nearly
up,
Feeling the cold steel against your temple.
Memories of things you've done since to fit in,
To come back to life and leave the bad dream.
Making yourself live in the present for your son and your
daughter;

Waiting for death.

Female players

Funny how they always say the blokes are players,
When in truth women play too.
Funny how they lead you with words dripping syrup,
But then stab you when you let them in.
Funny how something luscious can look so desirable,
Yet tie you up and cut strips off your heart.
Funny how she can try to make you look the bad guy,
While she struts around looking for new hearts to
break.
Funny how she hasn't the courage to walk how she talks,
Wish she wasn't played before by another.
Funny how these circles go on and on in ripples,
Until one has the courage to break them and stop.
Funny how the pain reaches out,
Greedy and dark.

Sad how she lets it live inside her.
Sad how she's fallen in love with it.
Sad how she wants to spread it.

Last thought before I sleep

You're my last thought before I sleep,
The warmth of your smile in my heart I'll keep,
Your musical voice echoes in my ear,
The drumbeat of your heart I hear.

And as the Sun sets I won't feel cold,
My past life will have no hold,
Because in my mind's eye I see you,
And now I know that 1 and 1 make 2.

You're my last thought before I sleep,
And in a sacred place your smile I'll keep,
And as I walk in this dream alone,
There's now a direction, a place I may call home.

And as the Sun sets I won't feel cold,
My past life will have no hold,
Because in my mind's eye I see you,
And now I know that 1 and 1 make 2.

Am I an old fart?

My arse fits my jeans or trousers
And I don't wear my pants around my knees.
I open doors for ladies or anyone.
I don't call everyone babe or hun.
I don't end every sentence with 'Innit!'
I tell the truth if you ask me a question,
Whether you want it or not.
I don't dribble when I eat or drink, yet!
I can still hold on to a fart with my buns of steel,
If I want to.
I can see wonder and joy in the smallest thing.
I don't expect everyone to like me,
And I won't hold it against you if you don't.
I am not afraid to state a preference.
I'm okay with a label if it helps you,
Just don't try to ram it down my throat.
I don't watch TV,
Preferring to try to live my life than anothers.
I can laugh at silly things,
Just like my kids,
Or splash them at the beach before they soak me!
I can still keep to the beat of the drum,
Or the bass.
I can smile at the happiness of others,
And celebrate their joy and well being.
I am not afraid to cry.
My undies stay inside my pants!
Am I an old fart?

When they come back

Will you stand by them?
The young who fall for you?
The ones who are chased in the halls of dreams,
By memories of things they have seen.

When you see old, haunted eyes in a young face,
Will you wonder why or just pass them by?
When they can't join your society,
For being able to see the truth of it will you cast them further
away?

Your world relies on fast food, newest cars and coolest
trainers,
Big brand names and the system's retainers.
Theirs on the disciplined bullet and the blind bomb.
Their young emotions locked in a tomb.

Most of them don't like the thought of having to take life.
Didn't like having to witness such strife.
Most of them went out to keep a peace,
Darkness and loneliness is now their disease.

Is it a job you could have done?
But you want the illusion of this 'freedom'.
Your world is grey, nature is white and black.
Will you stand by them when they come back?

Shimmoo

In the glow of the rising sun,
The colours of a rainbow.
The smile of an innocent child,
The laugh of the young at play.
The smile of a dolphin,
A family splashing each other on the beach.
The hug from someone who cares,
The protective embrace of a loved one.
The laughter of my son,
The impish behaviour of my daughter.
In all these things I remember you,
The gold in my heart....Shimmoo.
Be free little one.

Sentinels and the Ocean

Rocks like ancient sentinels.
Waves breaking upon them,
Reminding them of their vulnerability,
A cycle of thousands of years.
Where then will man sit within this cycle?
Will he disappear,
Never having listened to the sentinels?

Progression of a Soul

The truth of you streams through every word and sentence,
Like a record of your path and learning,
Evidence of scars and progression in the human condition.
Within you lies beauty and wisdom,
Far more potent than the material wealth society would have
you slave for.
And with it you cut the chains and freed yourself.

Hold your head up high when you are the only one,
Hold you head up high when you are the lonely one.
Hold you head up high when you doubt whether you
can take the next step,
Hold your head up high.

Your journey has been watched and you are blessed,
The ancestors rejoice in your coming of age,
They dance around the sacred fire and echo the drum in their
hearts.
Their hearts echo their love for you,
With it they give you their badge of courage,
Setting you free from the pain, watching you fly ... happy.

Spread your wings up high when you are the only one,
Spread your wings up high when you are the lonely one.
When you doubt whether you can make the next wing beat,
Spread your wings and fly!

Treat me to a smile

Treat me to a smile, one of yours,
It'll make me glow too.
Show me that you're a friend
And I'll show you the moon.
Send me flying over it
And I'll take you with me.
We can watch the stars together,
As friends.

Shooting for you

I shot for you and saw the stars
But I wanted to see the moon in your eyes.
I wanted to touch you in a way only I can.
I wanted to make you dance under the sun.
I wanted to make you laugh and share my world.
I still want to take you with me as I shoot for the moon.

Sleeping Thoughts of a Wolf

Come and walk with me while you dream?
See the world as it should be seen?
No wars or greed,
People living in a simpler way.
See the wolf wandering free,
Melting into the misty mountains.
See Grandmother Moon rise through the clouds
And hear my brothers and sisters serenade her.
Smell the leaves of the trees and the grass,
And a million things that you can't when awake.
Come and walk as a wolf a while?

Pain

You can't see with your eyes,
The pain that cuts like knives.
My eyes hide it from you for your sake,
Maybe for mine too,
Maybe I couldn't hack seeing my pain in your eyes.

Pain that tries to turn my soul black,
Sending me on that slippery slope,
Knowing if I fall too far,
There's no coming back.

Every day pushes me nearer the slope,
I sit here wondering how much longer I'll cope.
Every level of pain I endure,
Without complaint,
Unlike some character from an early evening soap.

Pain that tries to shrivel my heart,
Setting me up to be a freak in a glass case,
Seeing me curl up on the floor,
Longing for the time when I can depart.

Who do you tell when you're supposed to be a man?
When you've coped with everything as far as you can?
When tears make silent streams on your face?
They took back the ticker, now you're just an empty tin can.

Pain that leaves my senses numb,
Making it hard to see my way to tomorrow,
Silent screams lost in the abyss,
Leaving me ticking like a bomb.

Leave me with some integrity,
Don't take away my gentleness.
Don't leave me a callous shell,
Give me some hope, not pity.

Pain from opening scars in my mind,
Satisfying the system,
Only to be ostracised.
A slow, lonely death I will find.

Leaving the Storm

I went to her to say farewell.
The skies were grey and she wasn't settled.
I remembered my words to friends,
About always saying 'later' instead of goodbye.
So I promised to see her again soon.
I felt the caress of her essence upon my face
And in my hair as she soothed my thoughts.
She laid a gift at my feet in the shape of a heart.
A black stone.
Black, the colour of the peace warrior.
Peace she gave me as a parting gift,
And in my heart she will live,
Always, as mother to a son.
Time to leave the storm.

Boxes

Empty folded boxes lie near the cupboard door,
Where once there was a family.
Now there's just dust upon the floor.
Children's paintings on the wall there,
Keep calling back to me,
Reminding me of their laughter
And the way we used to be.

It's time to fill a box
And to take the memories with me.
Leaving behind the hard knocks
And concentrate on being free,
But to take my children with me,
So we're together the only way we can be,
For now ...

A day'll come tomorrow,
When they too'll be free
And they'll come and hang out without complexity.
That day there'll be no sorrow,
Just the love we three share.
They'll open the box I'll have saved for them,
With past happiness for us to share.

We'll journey on to tomorrow.
Together in some way,
Our bonds will be renewed.
The love that lasted will have saved us.
New happy memories will be formed
To help us on our way.

A wolf aged 44

I can see the journey so far,
The drive and energy of my youth,
I see the cub within,
Playing with boundless energy,
Serving and protecting,
Sacrificing my youth.
The hurdles I leapt in my vocation,
The arrogance of my youth,
Believing I couldn't be bested, save by a bomb.
The determination to be honourable at all times,
Even when those around me weren't.
Having my eyes opened to the realities of 'civilised culture',
Seeing that honour was their tool for us fools,
Something for which we would leap through fire!
As long as the goal was honourable.

Learning to live with the scars that now run deep,
Having learnt to read their lies.
Spending years trying to find justice,
That perhaps will never come ... but then it may.
Forged in the fires of my personal hell,
I became one that could 'do',
And ignored those who said I wouldn't be able to.
I stood judged by my deeds.
The Pathfinder emerged and the 'Wolf' was growing.
Facing my demons I climbed my Mountain,
Slipping and cutting my soul on every jagged rock.
Learning to balance,
Learning to love myself,
Learning to face myself in the mirror,
Learning to honour myself and my journey.

The demons still nip,
Life goes on.
I see people for who they really are, individually.
I don't fight for them anymore.
I go back to nature now,
The wolf running in the hills,
In and out of trees,
Feeling the sun on my fur,
The wind in my face,
The scent of nature fills me.
It's a different fight now.
I fight for peace within.
I learnt acceptance.
Acceptance of my disabilities.
Acceptance about the nature of society.
To be realistic about my goals.
To make sure the goals were achievable.
To be the best I can be within my limitations.
And now I can teach and share the medicine.
Protector,
Pathfinder,
Teacher,
The medicine of the wolf.

Veteran

When you've done your duty by Queen & Country,
When you've risked your all to get the job done,
When you've not taken the shortcuts or dodged the tough
jobs,
When you've been abandoned after your service finished,
When you've spent years trying to fit back into a society that
doesn't want you,
When you have to bare your soul to get help,
When your failing memory betrays what your needs are,
When everything is limited by the ticking of a clock,
When there are more casualties than the 'system' wants
to cope with,
When you're scored against each other rather than what
you need,
When your shyness keeps you in the corner,
When the system keeps moving your name to different
boxes,
When your mistrust of society keeps you in the shadows,
When you've had the treatment and the nightmares persist,
When all they'll suggest is to try filling you with pills,
When you go back to your empty home ...

You'll be a Veteran.

Romantic Fool

You see something in her eyes,
That isn't there for you.
But the longing blinds you to it,
And you make believe it's true,
That she'll smile your way,
And spend a little time.

There was a day you used to dream of a lot more,
That maybe she'd kiss you,
The way you've never been kissed before,
Or touch your face that gentle way,
And take you away on her smile.

But time has a way of wearing you down,
And bringing you to your senses,
Telling you to protect yourself,
Losing yourself within the fences,
And try as you might to keep on trying,
To keep the heart-light shining,
With every failed attempt you risk just giving in.

So you ask yourself,
Is it better to be safe and stuck in the fencing?
To not look into such eyes again and dare to dream a dream?
Or to accept your vulnerability and be a romantic fool?

Borderline

Falling between the cracks without a parachute,
Watching darkness envelop me.
Scraping my arms and legs against the granite walls.
Desperately staying visually connected with the light,
Only to see the darkness growing.
The suits turn their backs because I haven't let go completely,
'We can't help you until you've hit the bottom'.
Pride is a strong force within and arrests the descent.
The darkness is almost complete,
Save for the circle of the Moon.
Helping me to hang on.
I'm borderline.

Within the Amber

Within your amber I lose myself,
Or is it that there is where I find my 'self'?
Thoughts passed through your eyes and the tilt of your head.
Words don't exist, just thoughts and feelings.
No hidden meanings.
Soft whines dancing on the wind.
Harmony and inclusion in your song,
Ostracised no longer.

Behind my camera

Behind my camera I am safe.
An observer, no longer a participant.
Disassociated from the chains that bind me.
From the memories that can blind me.
From the trauma that haunts me.
From the society that imprisons me.

There is only the view from the lens.
Only the sense of connection with the Earth,
The spirit of the subject.
And the sense of calm that envelops me.
Gone are the chains ... for a while.

Live in the Sun

I live in the shadows of my past,
I try to play in the Sun whenever I can,
But I get burnt at times and retreat to the shadows.

Your presence drew me into the Sun again,
After a long absence.

Your voices caressed my soul in ways I can't yet explain.
Touching the strands of shadow that hold me back,
Making them release their hold on me.
Please be a real presence in my life?
I want to live in the Sun.

The shadows will always be there,
And the scars will need washing from time to time,
But you make me feel that I can do this...
And still live in the Sun.

Time to live again

With each word from your heart,
I feel the movement of mine.
Time to live again.

Absence

Ever find stillness?
The absence of all sound?
No emotion,
Totally alone?
Lack of peripheral vision?

Your eyes stop seeing.
The black starts on the outside,
And works its way in.
Everything stops,
And you begin to slide.

Nothing reaches you.
No sound,
No smell,
Nothing.
You're at the mercy of the darkness.

Sometimes it lasts hours.
It's still light outside,
When it takes you.
It only takes you when you sit in the silence,
Pondering your life.

In the darkness you awaken,
Trying to piece together the lost hours.
All I know is that it takes me
When I'm sat at home alone.

Autumn into Winter

All the leaves are off the trees now,
Some still lie amongst the grass,
Slowly decaying,
Feeding the soil with their corporeal shells.

Grandfather's light fades earlier,
Grandmother stays longer,
Bringing crystals to every surface I can see,
Cleansing the air.

The season of the first snow is upon us,
And my heart yearns for it.

The breath so cold
That it catches in my throat.
The sight of giant snowflakes
Flying on the breeze.

The sight of mountains and fields,
Covered in virgin snow,
Hiding man's atrocities against Nature.

Making things appear as they should:
Clean, beautiful, natural and harmonious.

Circling the Drain

Sitting here in silence, I wait.
The call for help unanswered.
One by one the chains that hold me to this existence snap
And I'm circling the drain;
My feet can't find the earth,
My fingers slide down the slippery slope.
I sit here alone, hope seems to have gone.

What do you do when the system's failing you?
Cause a scene, create a fuss?
These actions are alien to my persona.
I still recognise 'me' in the mirror.
I see the tortured child forged in the fires of rejection,
The teenager that escaped an abusive home.
I see the young man who risked his life to protect others,
Only to be burned for having a sense of honour.

The man that I became through countless baptisms of pain,
Was the man that fought hard for all those that asked it.
Using the energy made from the anger of injustice,
racism and rejection.
I fought hard for you,
To bring some justice to a corrupt society.
But when I have risked my all and sit here depleted,
As my spirit swirls in this whirlpool of pain,
As I see in my mind's eye that I'm being bruised and battered,
The skin scraped from my being,
My wounds raw and exposed,
The words 'help me' feel torn from my throat and die on the
wind.

Why won't you help me as I circle the drain?
I paid a price to help you.
You didn't have to ask, I gave freely.
All you seem to see is what I project from the outside.
I'm conditioned to hide my vulnerabilities and fears.
You only see what can be easily ignored or explained,
You don't take the time to find me.
Just another veteran circling the drain.

Time to connect

I feel the drum beating with my heart,
Calling from so far away.
Getting louder as each day passes,
Nearer to the time to fly.
I remember the warm wind on my face,
The scent on the wind.
I hear their songs,
Time to connect.

Acceptable Lies

I won't sneak up on you and tickle you 'til your sides hurt
with laughter.
I won't splash you by jumping high into a puddle we pass on
a rainy day.
I won't make faces at you when I see you frown.
I won't put on a silly voice in the middle of a dance.
These are the only lies I'll ever have told you,
And if you remember that,
The rest will always be the truth.

Thought before question

'Before asking the question,
Ensure you have the courage to hear the answer.'

My thoughts behind this piece are simple. People are too eager to ask about something personal but are not always prepared for the responses that come forth. Perhaps the answer will be deflating, offensive, enlightening, funny, sad, tragic even! The thing though is to be open to the answer and not to let it set off a knee-jerk reaction; especially if it's an answer that you really don't want to hear. If you don't want to hear the answer, don't ask the question. There are times when ignorance can really be bliss.

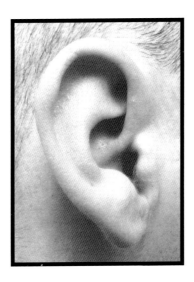

Searching

His eyes glisten in the light of the Moon,
As memories intrude upon the peace of the night,
Casting shadows upon the light of his soul.

He raises his muzzle and his sound echoes through the
mountains,
But no other voices join his,
And there is no chorus.
The silence of the mountain swallows his song.

He walks on, searching for his pack.

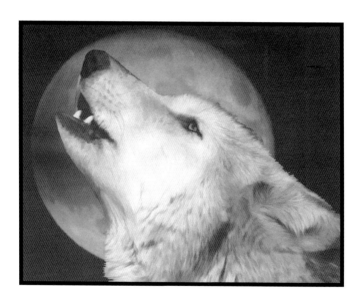

Mesmerised

Circling down, white and pure,
Living in moments, finding a link to ensure survival on
a cold wet land.
Different sizes, some float some soar,
On their journey toward the Earth.
Some go faster, caught up in the wind,
Some fall gently around the shelter of trees.
I stand there, a child within the man,
Tasting one that floats on my tongue,
Caught up in the rapture these beings create,
With their crystalline forms.
I want to lie amongst them,
Touch them, taste them some more!
I will always be a child in their presence,
Free, joyful and ready to play.

I gave you a Rose

I gave you a rose to see how you'd smile,
And you smiled from deep within,
Your eyes lit up and the glow encompassed me.

I tasted your lips to see how you kissed,
You gently drew me in,
And I sensed the passion waiting there.

I held you in my arms to see how you felt,
And we moulded into one.
I was warmed by your touch.

So what's with the bill for services rendered?

Live Life

Celebrate the warmth of companionship
And extend it to those that you know are lonely.
Keep the inner child alive,
Splash your friends in a big puddle or in an ocean wave,
Drop the fart that empties the room.
Tell jokes that make you laugh from deep down,
But not at the cost of another's pain.
Hug your friends.
Don't be afraid to smile at a stranger.
Don't be afraid to ask for help.
Don't be afraid to see a friend cry.
Don't be afraid to cry with a friend.
Walk well, walk free and remember to PLAY ... always!

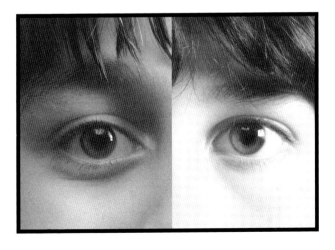

New World - Old Truth

Do you have what it takes to live?
To be free and to follow your heart?
Are you free to be that which you can?
Or are your ambitions chained by the new age?

Did you chain your heart to material success?
Did you sacrifice all that you once held dear?
Are you a product of this new world?
Stuck in a rut?

Do you teach your children the old ways,
Ps and Qs, holding open doors?
Do you teach them to speak from their hearts,
So their frustration doesn't choke them from within?

Is this shallow world what you really want to pass on,
Where monetary gains count more than an innocent
smile?
Do you not love your children?

Teach them to seek the truth.
Teach them to tell the truth.

Thoughts & Memories

Thoughts of Fistral and walks by the sea,
Golden sunsets and precious memories.
Thoughts of good times, laughter and fun,
Memories of beach parties and lying in the sun.
Thoughts of how easy life had been,
Memories of the jewels of life I'd seen.
Thoughts of how uncomplicated things were then,
Memories of events that made easy sense.

Bottles and Bricks

The sun is shining, the sky is blue.
The silence is sudden and tangible,
The birds stop singing.
It's as if someone pushed pause on the video.
As if by magic a crowd appears across the road,
Parents stand behind their children.
The first brick sails through the air towards my head,
I casually slip to my left and it misses me.
I focus on the crowd watching for a petrol bomb,
While signalling my oppo to call for back up.
My hand reaches down and I free the pistol from my
holster,
Chambering a round in case I see a legit target.

Parents are throwing bottles and bricks, teaching their kids
how,
The kids are smiling as they mimic their parents,
Echoing shouts of 'Feck off home, we don't want yous
here.'
'Catch this you English bastard!'
I smile to myself as I consider my ethnicity.

I continually scan all of them,
A thousand thoughts go through my mind at the same
time,
Am I cleared to open fire?
Not until I see a weapon or a petrol bomb.
If I have to open fire will the round go through my target?
Will it hit an innocent? The brain keeps storming.

I duck inside the shelter to my left and watch and listen,
Bricks, stones and bottles hit the shelter,
Glass splinters around me. I tense for a sprint toward the crowd.

I hear the patrol land rovers screaming towards us,
The crowd runs off behind the fisheries,
I give chase but they've reached safety.
The patrols hit the ground ready to chase the crowd,
Young, determined faces with their emotions locked down.

'Forget it,' I hear my voice say,
'We can't go into the Holiday Homes. Orders.'
I return to my post as the patrol heads off.
I make my weapon safe.
My oppo sticks his head out of the bunker,
'You okay'? I look up and smile the empty smile,
'Fuckin' peachy.'

The birds start singing again.

Living in a dream

Rise from the pain and dare to dream,
Shatter the chains of the past,
Wash the memories from your scars and fly!
Fly in your daydreams where you're free,
Unfettered by the nightmares surrounding your sleep.
Dare to be the soul that lives through the misery
And let the sun shine on you.

Flying for me, I'm flying for you,
Flying to see that smile of yours.
Flying for the dream, right into your arms.

Misunderstood and isolated,
You struggle to survive,
Looking for a reason to continue.
Find her in your dreams if she won't be your reality,

Live the old way where love meant something.
Dream your dream and let her fill your senses,
Swim in her eyes.

Flying for me, I'm flying for you,
Flying to see that smile of yours.
Flying for the dream, right into your embrace.

Don't drown in your present,
Escape to your dreams and feel the warmth.
Give yourself another reason to continue,
It's just another battle and you're a veteran,
Fight for yourself now and allow yourself some warmth.
Close your eyes and let her embrace you,
Let her smile envelop you.

Flying for me, I'm flying for you,
Flying to see that smile of yours.
Flying for the dream, come and warm me?

Hunter become the hunted

Cast from the light in shadows I now walk,
Watchful and weary, listening to their talk.
Wounded but not beaten, I ignore the waves of pain,
Calling on my last reserves to keep myself just sane.
Hunter become the hunted, in this little world I'm
stalked,
Remembering methods of survival from battles already
fought.
Neither villain nor a lawman now, locked up on my
own,
Removed from the board of life like some unrequired
pawn.
I listen to the chill night winds sending shivers through
my bones,
I sit here grateful to my mates for the letters from up
home.
Hunter become the hunted, lost but not alone.

Honouring the Boy

I remember going to my first unit by train,
In my best blues and white hat,
Shoes like mirrors,
Creases you could cut paper with.
A young man realising the ambitions of a boy.
Nothing was impossible,
Everything was up for grabs.
There were hurdles of racism,
But I'd overcome them so far,
The whistle and the two stripes were mine,
I couldn't be denied,
Having worked hard,
Pushing my levels of endurance.
Creating a new path for myself,
Where I decided the route,
Or so I thought.

I smile at the 5, 13,17 and 22 year old boy with fondness,
I let him fulfill his desires now,
Without internal hurdles.
As for the hurdles placed by society,
We'll go over or around them when we can,
And when we want to.

Ending thoughts

I remember the early days when I first had some awareness that something was wrong within me. It was about six months after I had left Northern Ireland; I was doing my training as a police officer in London at the time, in 1986. I was very afraid to talk about it in case someone thought I was mad and would section me to a mental health institution for my own 'safety'. I was aware of how such powers were abused in the 80s and I was working in the Metropolitan Police Force, an organisation that had inherent problems regarding racism in the ranks, which left me feeling more vulnerable.

The most difficult thing I have done to date in my life is to trust someone enough to talk about my PTSD. I was lucky to have had good care and support from the NHS and Social Services while living in Bristol and Cornwall. I had opened up about my PTSD in 1995. I did that for my son. He was a baby at the time and I had an understanding with my partner at the time that if we had any sort of health problem, we'd get it seen to for the good of the family.

The poem 'Circling the drain' was a direct result of my dealings with the NHS and Social Services in Nottingham since moving back to the Midlands. It was clear to me that the initial people responsible for my 'care' in the mental health team had no idea of how to interview veterans. As for Social Services, while I had a good social worker that understood the issues, her hands were tied with regard to appropriate support by her manager. The support offered, when it eventually came, was insufficient and inappropriate for a veteran who is hyper-vigilant and security conscious. It would actually have generated more stress for me.

Relying on the NHS to support you is a huge gamble, as care provision varies from area to area, as well as from practitioner to practitioner. There is still a huge amount of ignorance in Mental Health services in this country on the basics of interviewing someone with PTSD, as well as a lack of awareness around diagnosis. This may explain why providing appropriate care is such a problem.

Finding the support that you need can be an uphill battle. I had to lodge a formal complaint before I ended up under the care of a practitioner experienced in dealing with veterans with PTSD.

By reading this book you have walked in my moccasins for a while, caught between my words that express some of the turmoil of PTSD, as well as some lighter moments, and the freedom and sense of peace that photography affords me.

You will find more information about living with PTSD on my blog which can be accessed on my website: http://www.wolf-photography.com.

If you know someone who suffers from service related PTSD and wants help, please refer them to the list of agencies on page 64.

Good luck and look after the 'Self'!

Mitakuye Oyasin
(translates to All My Relations – A Lakota Prayer recognising one's relationship with all living things).

Villayat SnowMoon Wolf Sunkmanitu January 2010.

Organisations that can help UK Forces Veterans

Combat Stress (http://www.combatstress.org.uk)

Veterans UK (http://www.veterans-uk.info)

The Royal British Legion (http://www.britishlegion.org.uk/)

SSAFA (http://www.ssafa.org.uk/)

Help for Heroes (http://www.helpforheroes.org.uk/)

RAF Benevolent Fund (http://www.rafbf.org/)

Army Benevolent Fund
(http://www.armybenfund.org/index2.html)

Royal Naval Benevolent Trust (http://www.rnbt.org.uk/)

The Gurkha Welfare Trust (http://www.gwt.org.uk/)

NHS mental health support for UK Veterans
(http://www.nhs.uk/Livewell/Militarymedicine/Pages/
Veteransmentalhealth.aspx)